Side Notes
from the
Archivist

Also by Anastacia-Reneé

Forget It

(v.)

Side Notes
from the
Archivist

| *Poems* |

Anastacia-Reneé

AMISTAD

An Imprint of HarperCollins*Publishers*

The permissions and credits on page 129 constitute a continuation of this copyright page.

SIDE NOTES FROM THE ARCHIVIST. Copyright © 2023 by Stacey R. Tolbert. All rights reserved. Printed in the United States of America. No part of this book may be used or reproduced in any manner whatsoever without written permission except in the case of brief quotations embodied in critical articles and reviews. For information, address HarperCollins Publishers, 195 Broadway, New York, NY 10007.

HarperCollins books may be purchased for educational, business, or sales promotional use. For information, please email the Special Markets Department at SPsales@harpercollins.com.

FIRST EDITION

Designed by THE COSMIC LION

Library of Congress Cataloging-in-Publication Data has been applied for.

ISBN 978-0-06-322171-0

23 24 25 26 27 LBC 5 4 3 2 1

Contents

Section I.

Retroflect

attributes of the archivist:
-takes copious notes
-observes
-tries to remember
-says "remember"
-writes to remember
-remember?
-remembers everything
-underlines
-stacks
-folds
-sorts
-records
-takes pictures
-list   list   list   list
-holds secrets

/ Side Note /
archive: a collection of
documents or records or
poems or lists or thoughts or
music or breaths or blank spaces
providing information about
a womb, place, institution,
memory, ancestors, spirits,
community, coven, house, or
group of people.

Side Note:

we were trying to recreate the architecture of the bourgeoning disco scene, not because of the disco but because of the symbolism of the disco(ball), of the ball, of gay black men, of trans folx & of lesbian women in all sizes, shapes, & types holding them down. donnababa and babadonna embody a donna summer who is doctor, priestess, mother, father, holy ghost, and music. dani tirrell, writer, producer, choreographer, is *the* faggod.

the '80s (i was actually there) had a badrillion girl bands & boy bands & big group bands—either groups of blood family or chosen family, & they used to color coordinate outfits, do synchronized dance moves, & take airbrushed photos together & slap them on vinyl.

this all happened while donna summer put out "she works hard for the money," & at 13, i didn't fully know who the "she(s)" she was referring to were. even then i wanted to be donnababa. maybe in a big group & luscious lips & flipped hair but wearing a tuxedo & bow tie. in philadelphia that same year, i had to walk 5-6 blocks to the bus stop, & it seemed like all the people i encountered on my walk were getting thinner & thinner until one block was absent of all adult morning activity. only small children were running the streets & parenting smaller children to get ready for school.

by april, there were people walking around with pipes & strange items that looked like cotton & cigarettes all over the street. there were people holding boomboxes blaring girl bands & boy bands & donna summer. the news talking about some kind of gay plague. once, a tall woman approached me & told me to tell "them" "keep it in your pants unless you can make me dance." she laughed with her mouth wide open, & i thought her three teeth were white & beautiful & my 13-year-old nose loved the way she smelled—similar to red jell-o & granddaddy's aftershave.

that same year, i watched my schoolmate's mother walk him to the bus stop every morning in a long, brown hijab with lunch in hand, smelling like cocoa butter, & she would kiss him on the cheek & tell all of us "ma el salama," & we would all feel so acknowledged. i looked forward to this ritual. we all noticed it had been weeks since we'd seen him or his mother. on a friday jumu'ah, he was finally at the bus stop, & we who barely even talked to him asked where he'd been, & one of us yelled "and where's your mom! i missed her too!" & he said with a face as blank as a dry erase board, "she died of aids last week. i'm not going to hide it. if you don't want to touch me or talk to me, then don't." & i watched my bus stop friends scatter & move away from him. i stayed where i was standing & said i was really sorry. if only donnababa had appeared. like shazam. like pow. like alhamdulillah.

In the '80s

the cancer journals (audre lorde)
homage to my hips (lucile clifton)
tar baby   (toni morrison)

1980

& you didn't see the wiz until you were 10
& this is how you thought it might be
because even at 10 you could tell the future
because even at 10 you knew you'd be a teacher
because even at 10 you knew about the dream version
    of the east coast
because even at 10 you knew about peril
because even at 10 you knew you'd have to leave your
    dog & imagine you had a toto
because even at 10 you knew you needed some kinda fantasy
    to get you through

/ Side Note /
when harlem schoolteacher
dorothy (diana ross) tries to
save her dog from a storm,
she's miraculously whisked
away to an urban fantasyland
called oz. after accidentally
killing the wicked witch of the
east upon her arrival, dorothy
is told about the wiz (richard
pryor), a wizard who can help
her get back to manhattan.
as dorothy goes in search of
the wiz, she's joined by the
scarecrow (michael jackson),
the tin man (nipsey russell),
and the cowardly lion (ted ross).

1981

solllliiiddd & the goddess spun
herself to dizzy others
to make every bangle
& lace shudder
gooollllllddd
because you were 8
& didn't have the words
for energy or oshun or
conduit yet but the feeling
seemed like it could be
christmas day or new bike
or snow day or amusement
park or birthday cake or
swing or bbq all wrapped
up in her dress & irene cara
made disco libations
& when she said
remember my name (fame)
you did
think adults could live
forever
you did   think they could catch
the moon in their hands
you wanted your grandmother to
drape herself in solid gold
& now
you say
(*fame*)

1982

you wore your favorite hijab so tight
& brushed the baby hairs in a straight line   (first)
(before they called them edges)
& combed your forehead baby hair
with a fluoride-infused toothbrush
from the free lunch school packet
then crossed them all at the ends religiously
& that's when you realized
there are so many boundaries no one   can see   or touch

1983 (1)

after lunch salat
there were robust days
when you'd double dutch
with the full kids

*monday school lunch:
salisbury steak, kernel corn,
french fries, peanut
butter squares,
chocolate milk or plain*

your '80s
middle school
skeleton moonwalking
with halal hot dogs for dinner
& the smell of salisbury steak
on 6-section styrofoam plates
& maybe you call them robust
epidemic days
because there were also weak days
when you were all '80s ganged up
on by benetton colors
at every alley or street or stop sign
how your green clinging uniform never seemed to
blue or red well
bode well
or be well

not even facedown on a
                    tasseled   prayer mat

1983 (2)

there we all were
with cheerios
in hand, headed
to get milk

& all you eye spy'd
with your little eyes
were:
pictures of
girls gone
missing

all the parts of
the girls described
in black
& white photos

_____

file
born
abdicated from

you begged the lunch lady
for milk in a glass jug
to be oblivious
alongside your friends
who did not catch
the yellow bus or
know anything about
calcium-rich teeth found again

free lunch
or the stomach drop
of being

a latchkey girl gone missing

1984 (1)

you are a perfect girl
you do all the right things
you do not know about ___
you are carrot cake

the bodega in the farthest parts of your philly neighborhood
sold halal food & for this reason you were sent
to the farthest parts of your neighborhood
for carrot cake because carrot cake
from the halal bodega was much better than carrot cake
from the haram bodega & for that reason this bodega
was the only one you were allowed to walk *with a purpose* to

the bodega sold halal food
but you loved the "secular" music that vibrated
the cash register & the bean pies & miswak.
you loved to close your eyes
& pucker bonne bell lips like the
carefree no-hijab-pork-eating girls
& when the secular dj on the transistor radio
said *freak* on the radio

you didn't know what that meant
but you wanted
to be wound up
to be somebody's
freak. so when _____ grimaced   (at you)
you started winding & winding   (secretly)
inside pants
inside bloomers

underneath tunic
underneath slip
underneath hijab
every little baby hair slicked
from his vaseline of smooth talk
& when he purchased your carrot cake

you returned home as a *freak*
wound up & now haram

1984 (2)

you are a hairy-legged girl
wondering
about shaving her legs
who notices
when men talk
tina turner always gets   reduced
& there is magic
in black knees   black calves   black thighs
& a black woman
saying

                you better be good to me

      but

men who talk about
tina's legs
never grunt about ike
& all the times
she paid for
big wheels she kept on turning

1984 (3)

when mr. roarke strolled in
peppered hair & black necktie
a god-white suit & power
you wanted to ask him
what had he done with the
black girls from the island?
was there a top-knot-pony-wearing
black girl with living room carpet lint
as earrings riding on a red bike
in any of the scenes

(isn't this fantasy island?)

    (isn't this the place of ambiance & dreams come true?)

1985 (1)

you have seen the helicopter swarming
over the forbidden house of africa
& you know you are never able to tell
this tale or finish this poem.
it is a poem about philadelphia—
no   it is a poem about the house of africa
no   it is a poem about helicopters
no   it is a poem about bombs

last week (now) you saw a helicopter swarming
while you were sipping your coffee
& the lululemon ladies sunglass'd down in unison
to watch the propellers moving

& you almost choked on your own
memories of the helicopter dropping
bombs over africa
burnt hair in the middle
of your philly street

/ Side Note /
as the smoke rose from 6221
osage avenue, philadelphia,
residents watched through
their windows or television
screens in a state of stunned
disbelief. their city had just
bombed its own people.

on the evening of may 13,
1985, longstanding tensions
between Move, a black
liberation group, and
the philadelphia police
department erupted
horrifically.

1985 (2)

when bo & hope
had simulated
almost teen sex
on *days of our lives*
to peabo bryson's
"if ever i'm in your
arms again"
at 13 you wanted
that & you wanted
to be the
leather-jacket-wearing
bo holding hope
& awestruck
& you wanted to be
hope   so sure
so ready   bursting
'80s pop & summer
explosion
& when you heard
girls should never
have or be hope(full)
about boys—
that sex was a
thing you did to make
miniature adults—
you knew these days
were not about your life
& peabo bryson
wasn't making songs
for girls like you

1985 (3)

'80s shelter
meant the ywca &
when you hobbled in
rain as downpour of
young black drizzle
hipping a pouty 2-year-old
with clammy
fingers clutching
you like a blanket
(you) a sister in a
headscarf
brother as prayer
& now when you hear
shelter in place
you smell bleach
fruit cocktail
w.i.c. peanut butter
& nicotine from
your first friend
who blew perfect
circles of cigarette hugs
next to your
innocent small *x*'s
(two girls at the mercy of life's tic-tac-toe)
from the
bathroom stall

1986 (1)

when madonna talked
about her preaching papa

your 14-year-old
empty filled up
with the words *daddy*
& right from wrong
how you swayed back &
forth like your daddy
was a gospel singer
your body is a temple daddy

what it might feel
like to hear (your) daddy
               preaching

praying to madonna
that she would bless you

1986 (2)

in the '80s
your elders
asked if every
(body) was

on that stuff

those healthy
christmas bodies
now looking
halloween-bag &
tooth decayed

on that stuff

the stuff in the
'80s was:

food deserts
b-gyrls
the color purple
reaganomics
basquiat
kitchen table: women of color press
bombing of Move headquarters

girls wondering

what is the stuff any
(body) is made of

girls wondering

the stuff
(god) is made of

Post-Funk '80s

/ Side Note /

songs from the mixtapes
recorded from the radio

peter piper
mystery
do me baby
what have you done for me lately
how will i know
the bridge
the rain
6 in the mornin'
my adidas
meeting in the ladies room
wanna be startin' somethin'

|push record
& play at the same
time|

eric b is president
love you down
word up
kiss
it's my beat
that's what friends are for
nasty
no sleep till brooklyn
c'est la vie

the p stands for pay it no mind

the p stands for parade

the p stands for patron saint

Black Marsha (P) Johnson

1.

black marsha
i gathered you as
a bouquet
    center of
my table talk
& some of the
people there
tried to pick you
apart & i know
you would say

pay it no mind

black marsha
i see your rouge
reflecting black
at me in the hudson.
i want you to
know they
are (ok)

                    are the girls still
                    dying?

yes.

marsha p johnson
i think they want

to know more
about the duality of
black liberation

(ellipses or eye roll or shoulder shrug)

it's a price
well paid
& hard
to get free

2.

|*enter*|
  marsha p makes madea
& shanaenae build a stone wall
stone by stone
(when suddenly)
the. police.

ha
ha

madea's gun is useless

ha
ha

shanaenae says:

oh my goodness   (lipstick like a clown, fingernails waving)

3.

marsha p
looks so pretty
as a mermaid

&

madea keeps
trying to hum
marsha's song

&

shanaenae
keeps clowning

the sirens
keep coming

&

the sirens
keep coming

&

the sirens
keep coming

/ Side Note /
|**history** isn't something you look back at and say it was inevitable; it happens because people make decisions that are sometimes very impulsive and of the moment, but those moments are cumulative realities.|

4.

madea-   ha ha ha

shanaenae- ha

"*we were . . . throwing over cars and screaming in the middle of the street 'cause we were upset 'cause they closed that place,*" and "*we were just saying, 'no more police brutality' and 'we had enough of police harassment in the village and other places.'*"

would it be ha ha ha
                    ha ha
                           ha
(if)
shanaenae & madea were found
dead in two suitcases at a popular
park

how many trans women does it take
to _____

5.

dear madea

no matter what
they will still kill you
(too)

& everyone on set will
ha. ha. ha.
at your wig & dress
lying next to
a bouquet of bullets

(so funny)
new show idea

madea gets killed by police
madea gets placed in a choke hold
madea can't breathe
madea dies but gets forgotten
madea hangs herself
madea goes to the airport
& her id doesn't match the way she presents

ha. ha. ha.
hallelujer

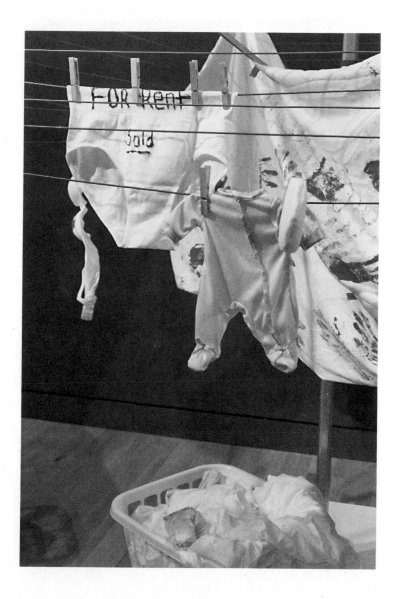

Section II.

Retrofuckery

> *insert scream here*
> —the archivist

(list)
1. my body is a forest
2. the rain forest is burning
3. i am burning—first my heart & then my eyes. each
   one smells of fish oil & champagne to celebrate/
   mark/ping/thumbs up
4. my body is an ocean
5. the ocean is covered with microplastics
6. i am wading through faux & replica. is this live
   or memorex? is my piss in 3d? is my uterus
   compostable? & who the fuck took my pearls?
7. dead babies

8. i had one
9. i shook in the shower & i shook in the kitchen & i shook at the doctor's & i shook on the sidewalk & i shook a stranger's hand—it was moving. there was an aftershock. a casual conversation.
10. there have been earthquakes & earthquakes & earthquakes

/ Side Note /
girls grow up

Her Life
(The Black Girl)
in
Unedited Episodes

pilot

in this episode
the black girl
contemplates:

am i a cannibal/am i cannibal/am i

all the ways
she boils her
rot & gums
her bliss away
how no two fingernails
taste alike & eating crow
holds the same
texture as a
lung. the black girl's
current catchphrase:
everything gives her
life because most
days she wants to live
& how can the black girl
live when she is
the butcher of
her own skin

|we might keep some of the original takes of her and air them as YouTube videos—she could easily become the next YouTube "it girl." for now, we are just reviewing some of the episodes & trying to figure out what parts of the black woman to throw away & what parts of the black woman to keep.|

episode (24)

at the black girl's job, she overheard coworker a.
tell coworker b. that she heard "kale is the new
vegetable" & black girl thought to herself, there
ain't nothing new about kale or collards or
mustards or soil underneath a black girl's
fingernails

at the black girl's second job, she overheard
coworker a. tell coworker b. how excited she
was to go on a camping trip to connect with
nature . . . & the tent & the living on the land &
the stars & the moon & the water & the quiet
& safety of "mother earth"

later on in this episode, the black girl walks a country mile
in her food desert just to get a bunch of fresh greens.
the black girl wonders   how it is that she has become
mother earth's stepchild, how it is she has to pay
for the moonlight & water,
how it is she fell like a shooting star,
how she cannot see her bright
in her mother & she focuses
on the boundless sky

|*when we're done, we'll change it up & cast a white woman with
soul. we originally wanted a black girl to sing erykah badu's "my
life" that we could then use to make it look like the soulful white
girl was singing "my life." we are still in conversation about that
& of course we will be completely transparent with the black girl
before we air the shows.*|

episode (16)

in this episode the black girl
has a raven's beak birded between
two gaps & when she smiles
a bone slips its calcified self
left of the veil mark
in the corner of her

lower lip

& she keeps breathing
even though she can hear death's
remix parading in the distance

& she starts singing "he's got the
whole world in his hands,"
but it's the devil who texts her to
say, "he can't talk right now he's
driving"

& the black girl is confused
about which is invested
in her the most—
good or evil

the black girl is wondering:
is hell the bathroom of heaven
or is heaven the attic of hell?

|fade in slow. close-up shot of the black girl's ass, then her lips,
then her hair (not her eyes) & play some kind of drum music. we

believe that makes regular blacks hocus pocus into africans (we need that connection for the woke white millennial). mix it up with a little rap & cue up a McDonald's commercial. the black girl has no idea we are filming her life & we like this because it makes it more authentic. we understand the main character is not a girl, but a girl is what we feel audiences will connect with better with the whole black girl magic.|

episode (27) *the most popular*

in this episode the black girl receives a letter in the mail informing her that her body (having been slowly historically erased anyway) will be a gentrified landmark

she has been asked to give her consent to (this) & she is supposed to say, "take my body as a living sacrifice"

|we plan to add maybe some gospel music & then make the black girl kinda look like she sorta wants to be gentrified & then we will like maybe have a white guy who will see her value maybe act like he wants her but not all the way & then we might add one of her coworkers to save her at this point & gentrify her later. we also might throw in a lump in her breast or something physical to keep audience members coming back to the next episode.|

episode (4)

*|we had to cancel filming this episode
because our main actress was so traumatized
about all the dead black & trans women
& i guess little kids too that she called in
sick today.|*

episode (7)

in this episode the black girl
ponders minstrel shows &
menstrual shows & all the
blood
blood
blood
in this episode//the black girl ponders sambo & mammy
& _____ & _____

& girls put down for asking about tampons & all that
   commercial
blood
blood
blood

|we are happy the black girl mentions these celebrities because
one of them is on tour & like the hot, hot black girl & the other
is popular with the generation z black girls. it's like . . . perfect
timing.|

episode (12)

in this episode the black girl
will hear from a ghost
it will tell her *boo* is an understatement
& white sheets & negligent lovers
get a bad name

the black girl will hum the dumb
ass song about cotton being
the fabric of our lives//the touch
the feel of cotton

this song will be remixed with a
negro spiritual (porgy & bess)
& she will get a paper
cut & think of a lynching
she will hear
boo boo boo boo boo boo
in the middle of her white sheets
& cover her face
to look like a klansman

& the highest part of herself will
wake her up & she will say
k
k
k
i'm up

|*wild day. the crew kept feeling like dead people were watching us. there was definitely some creepy voodoo shit happening on the set.*|

episode (5)

there is an episode in which the black girl is told she has to
first be raped, then be strong, then conquered, then be weak,
then split in half & afterwards she has to go to work.

|we thought about dyke-ing her up here a bit. but we need her to
be a soft lipstick lesbian. in terms of characters, we were messing
with the idea of like leticia musgrove meets cleopatra cleo sims
with a touch of aunt jemima.|

episode (23)

in this episode the black girl is going to visit paradise & the
big bad wolf steals her basket of vibranium & she runs down
the escalator back to her normal life & the white guy tells her
she gets to stay but has to pay a toll & her body mashes badly
these days & she keeps on whipping herself into shape & who
can ever get all the lumps out & who gets to decide the price
of the toll? or who gets to decide what takes a toll? or toll   toll
toll   spent

|we will play that old school song "bitch better have my money"
here and a clip from wakanda. maybe have the black girl subtly
do the wakanda sign across her chest.|

episode (0)

in this episode of the black girl (which will not air), where
the black girl conjures up her dead baby & the dead baby
conjures up the dead womb & the dead womb conjures up
its womb's lineage & the lineage tells the girl her baby has
joined the sea, that dead black babies all start out as black
girls & all black girls who are black girl babies start out as
god. floating.

|*we just find this too far-fetched. even if fantasy or sci-fi we can't
sell this.*|

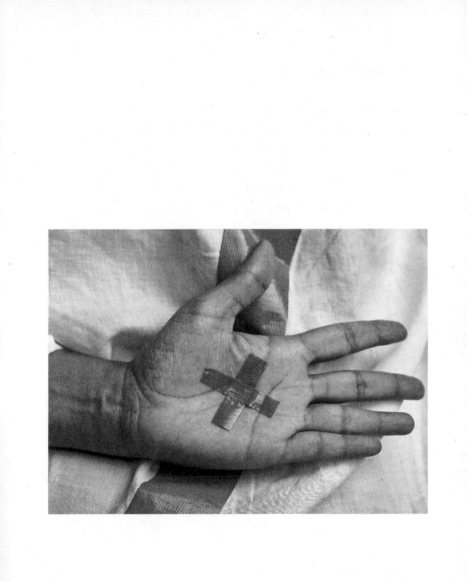

Section III.

Retrolove

q. what does one archivist say to another?
a. everything

(list)
come all ye
1. fashionistas
2. all ye pioneers
3. all ye sex workers
4. all ye poets
hiding as _____
5. single mamas
single mothering
yourselves.
this archive
is big enough
for you

faithful servants
of this soil
entangled
in oyster
shells & baby
teeth

brass horns
& green beads
& let me present
to you a blessing
as a baby in a
king cake

The Black Woman as an Altar

1.
lay your white flowers on
her altar. let them be thorny
& thick & full of insects to honor her life

1.a.
let them (the flowers) be fragrantly overwhelmingly to
    represent
the way she blooms across a
hardwood floor & cannot be
contained even inside a flared
nostril

2.
place or put or pour a glass of room temperature water
because the black woman is always seeking balance (ain't
she) a woman always told she's too hot or too cold has to be
excellent & never in between

2.a.
make the room temperature water all dreadlocked goldilocks
& just right. if the water spills let it run down the length of
the altar as a sign of continuous flow

3.
write a letter to womb   call it magical   call it home   call it
hers   call it god (but hide this letter in case the government
decides to step in)

3.a.

draw a sketch of stretch marks & label each one a new
constellation   make her navel a moon inside a moon inside
a moon & call that moon alpha

4.

if she died by a mob or a man or murder pray she will be
merciful that no one will be the weight of her own omega

Insomnia

when the house
is asleep
    i write my will
    & all my letters
    put them in a place
        someone will find
        tell people all is well
        because haven't we
            survived everything
            isn't pandemic just a
            long sterile word for

              history

              or

              systemic
              & learn

Hello Ma'am

the cardiologist is beautiful & for some judge judy reason
i don't think she has any problems with her heart.
i think it's the way she talks about mine in bless you
& pass the butter.
there is a frequency in the way she delivers small baby
    vowels
& swathes them with question marks
though they are statements.

you watch what you eat, right?
do you get plenty of sleep?
are there any stressors in your life?
because you know stress causes weird heart stuff.
you are limiting your fast food intake, right?
wow, so surprised your cholesterol is so low.

in the room, sitting next to an illustration of a normal heart
i have shared with her that she is my second opinion
my magic lamp
& draw-2 card.
but now i am
yelling uno uno uno because all the cards are dealt
& lying centered on the table
& she (still) after what feels like hours
has yet to meet my eyes
has yet to read my previous love notes
has yet to say my name.

Holy

your body is not halal
weak pillar no one will
pray for you
not once or twice
or even five times

your mouth an empty
prayer closet
your digits ashen off
in bean pie curds

if you were a call to prayer
your mother would call you
ayyub & let you drown
to watch you come to
life again

Libation Love Prayer (Neat)

this is a prayer
for the good foot
& the reserve nerve
for the pinky toe darkening
& the tiny lines holding each
binocular view
may you stretch time
& not be stretched to wafer
may your backbone slip
but not break
may you be crowned
& not crucified
copied but not erased
may your blood
rigor top shelf liquor
& mortis wine
may your name never
be followed with amen
let the ground sink
with your ase'

Do the Math: Corpse + One

to the corpse
who calls your name
a. no you will not go yet

---

b. there are children/dogs/cats/consciousness(es) to be
raised (still)
c. you don't want to be a dead poet

---

if she doesn't get a chance to grieve she will choke on her own
disappointment

d. no you will not go yet
e. the ground is not big enough to hold you
f. the sky not wide enough/ (but you can't swim in the sea)
g. it won't be easy to compost you (roughage + new shit)
g(1). you kiss with your eyes open
g(2). corpse never calls your name sweetly

---

say to the dead there's a future for your demons. we shall call
them angels

h. you like worms (but it's only because they have five
hearts)+

    i.   corpses keep saying your name wrong (anyway)

---

   ii.   *there the angel is*
  iii.   *lying on her back*
   iv.   *vulnerable*
    v.   *feet up rocking side*
  vi.   *to side & her*
 vii.   *heart saddled up*
viii.   *like a unicorn & kicking*

i. you cannot kill the ghost of a black woman//her soul a
succotash of sacred & somber too

& the humans
only tune in to
pretty angels
ones that
are polished
& confetti wings
bedazzled &
be-glittered like
beyond (say)
what might
be considered
normal

j/k. you don't know cpr//not enough to keep your own
ghost & corpse alive too

Close the Shades

if you haven't seen
the women of brewster place
you wouldn't know
about the game
the sidewalk-ers play
when we inch our shades down

how the ladies from the block
glance over glasses & make faces like
progressiveness has hot-flashed them

        & still we are
        the women of brewster place
        our windows wedged open wide
        enough to see
        our fingers locked
        on our altars
        enough to see
                wetness
        of water spilling
        from the vase
        holding flowers
        enough to see
        us sweating
        on our knees

        (praying)

/ Side Note /
in 1983, gloria naylor
wrote *The Women of
Brewster Place.* in 2021,
the archivist lived it.

I Will Order Myself

to be closer
i ate haitian food
today & it came
in a paper bag,
the handles
broken & sturdy.
i was so hungry
for it that i ripped
the bag open
& the food rumbled
& greens & carrots
looked like spleen
& plasma or
love. guts. guts.   guts.
all over the floor
like an earthquake
had come to   swallow
her own belly
& what
    what
    what can i do
but eat   all the   spices
stuck to my skin
like heritage or   dna
closer & closer
to my own mouth
to my own holler
& hoot
love. guts. guts.   guts.

Dear Young Poet

I. (mama)

poet, if you are a mama
you will not be able to
line-break your pee
underneath your spanx
& new target bra
(this is you bringing sexy back)
& skip to the bar to get another
whisky because there are
children eating god knows
what until you fling the door open
to trade in your toe-squeezing
poet-reading shoes for fuzzy socks
held hostage by the dog (who
is also hungry). there will be
no time to listen to your
peers deep think
an extended metaphor
or shit talk about other poets who
go over the expected time limit
& sweet thing
(mama)   the poets may not
not ask where you are or
if you are coming because
well you know she got them kids

II.   (heartbroken)

when you high step into the reading
looking immaculate & all done up
like a crown of sonnets, no one will know
there's a car wreck inside your chest
that you have spent your day as a wrecked
lonely siren wrapping gauze & disinfecting
your ache's desire. they will say you
look so good & you will forget for a
moment that you are just a round curb
walking & you will say things like
thank you i try
cheese with such fervor your ribs
push in so you don't spill out
right there in front of the podium.
          but someone
dear poet will see sorrow in your lipstick
& you will read the best damn poem
& it won't be about heartbreak because
who needs more poems about
dead birds & prince songs gone wrong

Wrapped

boding body
neo-antique
frame of enamel
& moles
& whisky
stack of
regenerated
failings
windows of grace
of miniskirted hymns
love songs & earlobes
& butchered meat

/ Side Note /
q.
if the human body is the product
of two animals, can anyone
really be a vegan?
q.
if they tell you your body is a
temple & you prefer a masjid, is
your body not worth prayers?

An Estate Sale of Your Memories

i. memory prep

skate into the memories barefoot or ballerina or bone-
sucked. there are many stories. there are piles & piles of
your memories panorama-ed about/around/all over/all
through   some piles piled in perfect circles whooshing
like swirls on a 7-year-old birthday cake   some messy like
dormant fuckery or matted hair or stovetop grease way under
or below a bluesy fire burning calamity orange

there are some nameless piles of things   of (stuff)
of whites of colors of delicates
that you think do not belong (together) like car crashes & 2 a.m.
assaults & you say to your memories' estate keeper (why is
this here with this)   & there is a kaleidoscope'd you that
is not you telling the glasses you that is (you) that this pile is
correct   just the way it is to go on/check out the next
pile & you find yourself wanting to clean this pile up & you
ask the memory keeper where is the bag   the bag
to shove the memories (in) where is the bag to tuck the
memories in bed & pray they sleep through the night & the
memories' estate keeper tells you (baggage) there was so
much baggage & the baggage has to be cleaned out cleaned
away cleaned up cleared & this is when she
suggests to put them on special clearance. the baggage will be
sold for very little. all your
hold-back & torture will go there (she centers you in it)
upfront/as people walk in

ii.

when you sift through your memories & put them (up)
for sale you decide to begin as most things do at the end at
the bottom of the cup of the bowl of the barrel where the
bitter bitter is or the sweet sweet & you will count on your
memories to sell themselves like sex or drugs or prayers. you
will count on them to be shelved perfectly so that onlookers
will want to purchase them right (away). there is the one that
becomes two that becomes three that becomes four & you
decided to lump these all (piled nicely) as a bargain not as
clearance (make it clear) that there are four memories (hear?)

& you too can walk away with this baggage

iii.

~~there is a ____ pile. this pile says don't touch. says moon. says~~
~~a uterus hanging outside a self-imposed coat hanger & a stag~~
~~of a tree (not rotten) says buyer beware & there is no place~~
~~like home~~

the open rooms down the hall

there's a room where the memories are playing dominos
with each other
all your bones being slapped on the table & you are laughing
at the way you
can see the dots being put together like how 13 is kind of
lucky &
how money don't grow on trees

there's an attic in a room inside a room where the negative
voices feast on
directions & they say things that make total sense because
it's inside an attic
up   there
& because it's   up   there you likened it with god//
how you thought god was telling you all
the things that were wrong with you

Low & Leaving

once an acupuncturist with
needles in her teeth told me
my qi was low & leaving

qi low & leaving
i guess   you are no better
than my father deciding
to split from the thing he
founded from the thing on
which he gave pieces of his life

father low & leaving
what an   unbalanced body
you created   then tipped
what a soul   sucking
dead man still poking
holes   in my head

Rest Well

1.
i lie in bed and fidget my hair to cornrows
as a meditation on sickness
about what the body decides is big or small sick
on what the mind decides is a crater or valley

the cornrows are not straight
& i delight in that fact imagine myself a child
running through a maze of cornrows
snagging my favorite shirt on the thicket of blackness

when the pain rushes in again i meditate counterclockwise
& untwist
the cornrows & imagine me as that same child getting lost
in a billow of blurry trees

2.
i considered dying in my sleep
my heart so full of love it becomes
a candy crush of flooding in each little chamber

i considered what the odds are for
you know a person (like me)
a person carrying persons on her
                    back
how far can i swim (like that)
how wide can my ripples be (like that)

i considered how much i need to be watered daily & how my
mouth might hang open (like a fish) in the form of a long *o*.
that is to say home. that is to say lone. that is to say row. that
is to say moan.

No _____ Left Behind

woman
you wonder
how many
pieces of yourself
(dank underground)
how many railroad tracks
have held your memoir

under its bleeding gums
you, woman who
has never been
a child

roaring '20s
in your diaper &
george orwell
in your hair

you beloved
you begotten
bantering of possibility

you proposal
of apocalypse
wife of uncertainty

farmer of forgotten land
yes, you (child)
the woman.

Arrest: Cardiac

(Atatiana Jefferson's father dies weeks after daughter was killed by a police officer)

/heart/		beat
attack		beat
attack		beat
attack		beat
attack	/systemic/	beat
attack		beat
attack		beat
attack		beat
attack		beat
	attack attack attack	beat
	attack	beat

Usher in White

i am the usher of:

night women

day omens

the circadian rhythm
mash-ups in a gyrate
of open-eyelid prophecy

                    women

the fire under the tongue
& next time   women

the giovanni's room
pepper sauce
tears   women

the trapp crackle pop
vinyl   women

the freaks come out at
night   women

the *my pronouns are
they/them/unicorn*   women

the southern spit on top
of midwest drool by way of
soup joumou   women

the bbq & jazz crazy little
women   (women)

the forgive but don't forget
heal you with herbs from
my garden

                                                       women

the don't ask my neighbor
but you better ask somebody

                                                       women

salt across the
threshold + garlic
at the door

                                                       women

i had an abortion
on my birthday

                                                       women

grudge holding as you
cover me with dirt

                                                       women

black candle & release
cleanse on a new moon &
burn you with sage

                                                       women

Calling In Black Today

i'm calling in |black| today.
actually, this whole weak.

i'm calling in |black| this weak.
send your work emails with not
one ounce of regret to my white
colleagues

inform your payroll that i was already
on my reserve nerve—that losing pay
was already covered by the weak(end's) blood.
i wept.
you are saved.

i'm calling in |black| this weak
find another |black| body
for the front of your brochure
maybe a tanned beauty
for your all-important grant & sugar cane.

Home for the Holidays

for easter the girl wanted to be a soft blue hard-boiled egg,
easier not to touch or feel a thing, easier to fracture herself a
splint for all the egg whites her yolk has ingested

for christmas the girl wanted to be the ornament on top—any
shape any color anything but hanging from the middle of a
tree. what girl wants to repeat a lynching what girl wants her
head decorated & cocked to one side against a starry night?

for mother's day the girl will be her own womb & die when
she is a baby (inside) & she will say it was a drowning—an
inaccurate way to hold such a big fish in a small sea

Black Girl Tarot Cards

*minor arcana

you minor girl. your center, the most devout thing since a
nomenclature

let this house be a deck of the highest empress card you
ever did not see

spread   splayed

sienna light through a flickering flood of saints turned
aints cuz count it all joy to the little you of all big yous (you
talkin' bout me?)

splayed   spread

your hands, a silver glimmer of god's gamma rays. i can see
you just as clear as the memory of yourself you keep in your
black hole & this is the gravity of time

who can say they haven't tried to defy (it)
who can say they never set a trap for a mouse

who can say they never were a tripe of a vegetarian
contradiction in an alleyway full up on well-meaning
thieves

you major girl. all your pre & post distilled in a little legacy of
last lifetime's laundry list of furloughed misshapen moons

& interstellar denials. tiny little mishaps hiccupping solo like
a distant star glistening from your whole life's oceanography.
you've been the fool

& the high priestess & emperor'd tons of love/less lovers in a
yellow chariot driven by your own hoofs &

breast. who even knows (but you) girl how much strength it
takes for a hermit to live through death or sparrows beaked

no   to hang in the bounds of justice in your skinful
temperance bless sun & the stars be just a piece of

your wheel of fortune of a whirl

THE BLACK MARKET
CANDLES $3
ANGRY BLACK WOMAN HAIR $5
HAIR OF MURDERED BLACKS 1955-2020 $1500
JAZZ ALBUMS $35
SMUDGE STICK $10
PRECIOUS PELVIS WHOLE $3000 SLICES $150
AFRICAN AMERICAN BOOKS 5 FOR $100
MARKET COFFEE WHOLE BEANS $12
EYE CANDY 5 FOR $5
BLACK MAGIC MIX BLOOD, SWEAT & TEARS PER VIAL $50
SAGE BUNDLE $3
REPARATIONS INCENSE $60
APPROPRIATIONS INCENSE $5
INCENSE HOLDER $4

Section IV.

Retroblood

(list)

things no one ever tells you about adulting:

1. pain can be a scar or a beauty mark but it's always permanent
2. your highest self has levels of height
3. self-care does not lead to self-actualization//being selfish does not always make way for self-care
4. when you are young, they will love you for having an old soul. when you are older with that same old soul, they will see you as a light but not in neon or disco or angel
5. if you lose a baby or have an abortion there will be a hole to heal//the christians will feel more compassion if you lose your baby & the _____s will respect you more if you have an abortion
6. your ride or die will be anxiety & you will break up with anxiety often//your ride or die will be anxiety & you will make up so many times//anxiety will save

you from yourself//anxiety will ruin you (you will
doodle or knit or clean or cook to make it be a good
thing)

7. you will not forgive your father//you will forgive
your father//you will think father & (farther) are so
similar

8. you will beg for amnesia//you will try to
remember//sometimes within the same hour

9. you will try to hide all the languages you speak,
including body

10. you will live near a racist but they will bring you
freshly baked cookies, attend diversity meetings,
& ask you if you know a black celebrity. you will
answer _____ but never eat the cookies

Shivering Womb

some days my own womb shivers at the thought of
my black-ass children being thrown
against any wall
on top of any car hood
inside an open ground

& it feels so lonely
in every audience
in every café
in every bookstore
in every park
in this city
in this state
at every poetry reading
in this country

how i wish i could take in statistics & visuals as only sad
    collected data
wish my suck of teeth & saliva-hurt was not woven into
    my gut like natural flora
how i am suddenly jealous of one's imagination or this so-
    called learned empathy
what might it feel like to be able to shut off a cell phone
what might it feel like to only panic for myself
to only think of my own attack

Casual Conversation

the woman shares with me
her assault & does not give
me a heads up of what is to come
& there my fight or flight is
bouncing on her knee. then
the next thing i know she
blurts *the rapist looks a little*
like my son—but she didn't mean
it (that way). it's just the skin
& eyes & hair & height similar
in her fair recollection

/ Side Note /
the archivist states:
there were juvenile songs
trapped in our ears
we were capturing
sweat in a time capsule
like a firefly   lighting
up & stall stickied-
wet with *fame.*

Wailing Bench

they say the whale
has so much more
brain than humans
but if most of my
lineage has been
drowned in the ocean
then is the whale
swimming in her black
brilliance
brilliance it seems can
drown you & how much
or how little is no exception
& that's why i imagine some
people speak with a gurgle
some people float on by
dressed as a life preserver
but actually just dying to
swing themselves around
your neck
your neck
is already tired
from _____ & so it is. <like>
seeing your own sister/self under
water only to fill your own
mouth with the wetness of hell

/ Side Note /
"but when we really delve into
the reasons for why we can't
let something go, there are
only two: an attachment
to the past or a fear for the
future"
—marie kondo

Kondo Living

you want to let systemic racism go, but you are attached to
the past of it & lord(t) knows what will happen to the tangled
ropes it knots in the future & you are left here hanging &
then _____ _____ tells you that you can do it & she is so
reserved & pretty & has a daughter who likes to fold laundry
& you want to ask if you should fold dirty laundry too//if
shoving a shoulder in on both sides (this is how you properly
fold a shirt)

               is a true gesture of letting go

you want to put all the systems of oppression in one pile

all the internalized classism in a pile

you want to put the patriarchy pile into two piles because
there are lights & darks & you are forced to sift through
them evenly

visible mess helps distract us from the true source of the disorder

you want to declutter the womb you thought belonged to you
& send the bent hangers & old gloves away

tidy by category, not by place　　　(but gentrify in the shape of
a box)

- portland, oregon 58.1%
- washington, d.c. 51.9%
- minneapolis 50.6%
- seattle 50.0%
- atlanta 46.2%
- virginia beach 46.2%
- denver 42.1%
- austin 39.7%

you want to gather up the bricks & pods from the gentrifiers
& tell _____ _____this is what you want to let go of &
she will say (yes) she can help you
she can wash your life & create white space again

Roughing It

1.

poverty: it's what's for dinner
poverty living is the new thing
have you done your poverty thing today?
lack is the new _____/\

2.

your coworkers are so proud of the way they lasted in the
forest for a whole weekend without cell phones & heat   /\
how it felt so good to sleep under the stars & be adorned by
orion's belt/\

3.

if you live a life of a minimalist by default, what is your
capacity for maximum joy? /\most everything you own you
can hold inside your hand. should you let it go? should you
downsize your homeless stairs? which holds more joy: a
stranger's leftover coffee or an unopened can of sardines?/\

Ask Siri

& cancer says to siri:
you know too much about me

        & siri says to cancer:
        a person who has an
        excessive interest in or
        admiration of themselves

& cancer spends 3 chemo sessions
talking about how he's not about
that life & how he is not
a narcissist & how he does not
think the world is all about him

        & siri says to cancer:
        (of a person, action, or
        motive) lacking
        consideration for others;
        concerned chiefly
        with one's own personal
        profit or pleasure

/ Side Note /
south carolina police are now
searching for the remains of a
missing 5-year-old based on
their interview with the lead
suspect

Yonder

is the ache a fig
a rotting peach
a bruised plum
pluming
how deliciously rotten
can it be
the confection
of a black swan molting
her remains
almost found
in the cotton candy
of america's
freak show
is it—
honey
bbq sauce
a placenta
boiling
in a bacon
broth of
new plasma
because . . .
step right up
all bets are
swimming

all cards are
hands down
& poker face
from the
man
on this
simmer of a
commercial
a break from
triggers
& ducking
again & again

/ Side Note /
the archivist does
not collect white
tears but sees them.

Ash

the rubble—
there rose the
chapter made of
trips completed &
fake mosquitos
& songs cloaked in
bad couplets
& black bodies black bodies
& black bodies black bodies
& for this reason
if you were born
in the spring of
2020 you learned
words like:

pandemic/ rona/ mask/ wipe/ protest mask/
quarantine/ racism/ overdose/ shot/ killed/ bleach/ murders/
no hugging/ remote

before you
could even
say your own
name

Sculpt: The Archivist (278)

the sculptor
envies the sculpted
that is to say
the sculptor
wants to achieve
frozen perfection

to sit as a bust
in refrain
to be seen from
all sides as a type
of god

& like the ants
& aphids
the sculptor
wants to revel
in seeing herself
survive

to be a slab
of un-toppled stone
to stay alive
even when the
ball & crane give
no warning
even when
do not enter
breaks

Stop Saying the World Is Not on Fire

here we are outside with our masks on talking about insignificant things (they are catching me up on all things 20-something) because the world is crumbling all around us. (we keep shifting our poses while sitting dodge dodge dodge.) the world is not on fire. incense is on fire. fireplaces are on fire. teakettles are on fire. the world is a volcano eating itself (& us) & we are social distancing mom/kid time & blood blood is coming out of our mouths. blood is breaking our promises & digging at the waxed umbilical cords tethering us to our ancestors. we are laughing because it may be the last time we grin. grin & bare it. grin & bear it. & when i go to hug them ||i cannot|| & if the foot of racism suffocates them, i can't (either). i raised them (tiny gods), but now they feel ghostly floating because they keep being haunted by _____ & i keep wondering if they might tweet up missing or if i will be a new addition to an altar. god i want us all to (be) but not to become a part of the roster (mama) god: to say the world is on fire is saying it's a paradise. i blew them kisses, but i felt ash on my lips. my lipstick print like an orange peel against two perfectly split endocarp.

Semantics

potato
potata

tomato
tomata

corner store
bodega

top
shirt

soda
pop

bathroom
restroom

far
yonder

date
court

bathe
shower

living room
parlor

gentrification
repurposed neighborhood

hate speech
right to free speech

master bedroom
master's bedroom

Home

cheers to the man who can sleep unfettered & the house
protected by gingerbread houses

for the bird box dangling from the old tree above the freshly
painted white fence & the amazon-smelling tricycle on the
newly cut grass

for the mother-in-law house in the sprawling backyard next to
the garden growing wild with good health & the rocks flown
in from Italy

when you spill your drink:

cheers for the bones jenga'd below

One More Thing

I. possible names after (this):
    a. kovic
    b. covica
    c. ckovicarona
        1. you start to dream of babies born with tiny hazmat
        suits on & the doting mother folded on the bed like a
        yellow trash bag & there might be procedures like (this):
            a. wash that baby's hands
            b. put the baby in the bag &   cover the baby &
            just poke a hole for its lips
            c. text the mom & tell her she can hug it from a
            a distance while the new bundle is welcome to the
            height of magnified freeze

/ Side Note /
we keep going to the store
getting things we think we
need   hand sanitizer
if the end comes who can
hand sanitize any government
away
wipes
clean
so many babies created in
heavy rubbing of elbows so
many pandemic children
conceived coming up on a
quarantine hand sanitizer

Are We There Yet

-negro hymn

negro (him)

change gone come.   *(yes it is)*

we
shall
o ver commmmeeeeeeeeeee.   (tear gas)

martin is it coming?
can i order a new cheek online?
my current cheek is not compostable & does not come with
  a filter
if i am pepper sprayed while i am peaceful does the change
  come?
if i am pepper sprayed & not peaceful does the change come?
(shoot)

(hmmmmm)

When You Are Asked How You Are Doing as a Statement & Not a Question When the Real Question Is, While You Are Bleeding Out, "Can You Tell Us What We Should Do to Bandage Up the Blood?"

your life is a meditation on asphyxiation & keep it moving
your days spent explaining to progressive organizations
why they need to make a "statement"

why they need to say a thing   how they have chosen to be
                                    the glossy mouth of white talk

with no worry of running out of breath

your life is the overlap of do something
& help
of make a difference
& rot while the world
doesn't ask you why
& doesn't sing
any songs you know by heart   at the end of the day
   you soak your feet in a tub of isolation

you sweat praise as grainy as sand
& when the _____ organization decides to just get *caught up
in bad timing*

or when the organization
just can't muster up a statement

you will be the website picture they use
as a sample of niggers to be lynched
by the neck of their names

Aunt Jemima
Is the Picture of the
American Dream

Aunt Jemima as the
White Girl's Auntie

& the white girl grew up
with fangs
in aunt jemima's neck
& the white girl likes her
black women
savory & sweet
wants to chew black women
into pieces
& crunch silhouettes
on her tongue
what a mouthful
in the way she was raised
how she believes
all the aunties are hers
all aunties should kneel
to her kicking feet

/ Side Note /
"during donald trump's
campaign rally in arizona
on tuesday (june 23), one
speaker complained about
the 'cancelation' of aunt
jemima and called the syrup
brand's trademark 'the
american dream.'"

Aunt Jemima as Auntie

& if my aunties were cured with salt
all our tears would swim around
each mermaid swimming
all of our eyelids pressed against each collarbone & spine

& if my aunties were cured with salt
i too would have a cure for the ways in which
we are ravished & preserved
for ivory carnivores inhaling the land

i tell my children & the women
make a salt circle around your body   place
the salt under your tongue   snug
next to the entrance of your
soul's gaping hole   shakeshake

/ Side Note /

"aunt jemima was canceled.
if you didn't know, nancy
green, the original, first aunt
jemima, she was a picture of
the american dream," student
reagan escudé told the crowd.
"she was a freed slave who
went on to be the face of the
pancake syrup we love and
have in our pantries today."

Aunt Jemima's Crown

& i greased
aunt jemima's
scalp parted in
tiny circles
we low whispered
about _____ people
trying to make
her smother her own crown
about _____ people
stuffing her in boxes
about _____ people
using her soul as batter
& then flipping
her all around.

_____

/ Side Note /
"she fought for equality,
and now the leftist mob is
trying to erase her legacy,"
she continued. "and might I
mention how privileged we
are as a nation if our biggest
concern is a bottle of pancake
syrup."

Aunt Jemima as Gold Dust

& aunt jemima
was pushed over
while the proud
boys tripped on
cubes &
they each took
one good turn
erasing the lines
in the palms of
her hands, saying:
isn't it great to
be here again
(reagan-esque'd)
isn't it good to see
our history bubbling
around the edges
golden brown
& ready to turn

/ Side Note /
often, "old Aunt Jemima"
was sung while a man in drag,
playing the part of Aunt
Jemima, performed on stage.
it was not uncommon for
the Aunt Jemima character
to be played by a white man
in blackface.

the monkey dressed in soldier
clothes, old Aunt Jemima, oh!

oh! oh! went out in the woods
for to drill some crows,
old Aunt Jemima, oh! oh! oh!
the jay bird hung on the
swinging limb, old Aunt
Jemima, oh! oh! oh! i up with a
stone and hit him on the shin,
old Aunt Jemima, oh! oh! oh!
oh, carline, oh, carline,
can't you dance the bee line,
old Aunt Jemima, oh! oh! oh!
the bullfrog married the
tadpole's sister, old Aunt
Jemima, oh! oh! oh! he
smacked his lips and then he
kissed her, old Aunt Jemima,
oh! oh! oh!
she says if you love me as I
love you, old Aunt Jemima,
oh! oh! oh!
no knife can cut our love in two,
old Aunt Jemima, oh! oh! oh!
oh, carline, oh, carline,
can't you dance the bee line,
old Aunt Jemima, oh! oh! oh!
—billy kersands (1875)

/ Side Note /

mammy
aibileen clark
& nell carter

Aunt Jemima Travels
to Victoria's Secret

& aunt jemima
asks for a proper
bra fitting for
(her breast)
& lifts the curtain to
find a line
of white babies

their oval mouths
frozen & fish hooked
& waiting

(her breast)
smashed together
nipple & sway

Section V.

Retropresent

q. who hugs the archivist?

a. _____

(list)

how to disappear/go unnoticed/not be heard (unless you are angry)

1. be black
2. be a woman
3. be a black woman
4. be over 30
5. be a black woman over 3o
6. be a mother
7. be a black woman over 30 mothering
8. be queer
9. be a queer black woman over 30 mothering
10. weigh over ____ pounds
11. be a queer black woman over 30 mothering weighing over ____ pounds

Crest

here

your body has poured a chalice so full your nerves runneth
    over
& your eyes vibrate bronze & cracked pewter
say to each molecule rocking back & forth

rest

to every artery & chambered conch
to the blood cresting & vessels mouthing   (the tide is out)
to each sense sanitized with woe
to tiny specks of deliverance in each eye
in the sunflower'd centers of every
fibroid or jellied cyst
& the alice coltrane of every tumor's melody

rest

here

Winter Is Coming (but First Fall)

in the fall you gather your goodness
to hide it from yourself so that you
will have a stash of grace in november
& you are not a hoarder by nature
but you will take the compliments you
receive & stack them up like old plastic
i can't believe it's not butter containers
you will take the hugs strangers pass
on to you & shove them in a duffle bag
you will spreadsheet every time you felt
a warm fuzzy, warm embrace, or warm milk
made by the hands of someone else
in fall you gather your goodness
to hide it from yourself so that you
will have a stash of grace in december
& you are not a hoarder by nature
but you will take heart-to-heart talks
& hang them gently on the tree of life
in the place you call the living (room)
you will wrap your children's well wishes
& tie yourself in a neat red bow & when
winter comes (& it will), you will give
yourself these hoarded things in increments
so as to make it during your birthday
& the month they call romantic
surely you can save up 60 days' worth
of goodness. surely mercy & goodness
last forever & ever amen

Black Hole

1. when the scientists say the black hole that shouldn't even be a black hole exists & is larger than any black hole i hear cool dirt being shoveled in my ears. it sounds like plastic in the ocean.

2. i have always loved the color black, not because it's beautiful but because it's mysterious, or not because it's mysterious but because it's overpowering or because it's big, or i love the color black because it is not in the rainbow & i am always rooting for the hue no one sees.

3. once i imagined my womb as a black hole & a daughter i had got sucked in & lost forever & another daughter i didn't know got sucked out, & if my black womb is a black hole, then the black hole could be a womb, & that makes sense when the scientists say the black hole that shouldn't even be a black hole exists & is larger than any black hole because i mean (history).

4. what if there are _____ women, mismatched socks, lost little girls, gunshot victims, keys, reproductive rights, earring backs, memories, & chapstick in the black hole.

5. another reason i like the color black is because in the 70s, people gave 5 on the "black hand" side, & i miss doing this & the missing gives me a black hole as if it never existed, as if i shouldn't really exist, not because i am beautiful but because my hue is invisibly overpowering & i mean (history).

Cloven-Hoofed Fortune Teller

the deer pauses
to see through me
outside my window
inside my life

after some crying
about a little doe
moving on
i see myself
as a crest of moon
inside her eyes

a fortune
she may be telling
as a gleam
or glint
or fire
she is trying
to make

& i realize
we are not
much different

both of us ignoring
what's behind
& up ahead
waiting to run

Yoga/Not Yoga (Flash Poses)

surrender i.

this is where you lie straight
like a hot dog
but on your back
& yell *fuck i. just. can't*
three times with your
right or left hand (no judgment)
in the cleansing
fuck you finger position. careful not
to extend the middle finger too far.
let it naturally rise enough just to be seen.

surrender ii.

this is where you will lie down
on your stretch-marked stomach
kick your feet into the air & chant

i just. can't
i just. can't
i just. can't

you will begin to feel a release that
starts in the middle of your forehead
& travels down to your throat. you may
cry or you may scream or you may feel
yourself saying things like:

i don't give a shit about any of this motherfucking
shit & fuck this & fuck that & who in the hell even

gives a fuck about _____& why me & how could
& but now & but now what & higher power or tree or
bar of soap i. just. can't. you'll have to clean this mess
you could potentially hear things that sound like:

give up
shut up
hold up
suck up
sit up
pick up
push up
fuck up
take up
shape up
screw up
get up

                                        surrender iii.

you will know for-sure-for-sure as in damn right if at the
end of this you have no more energy & you are sort of
dry heaving or suffocating your face inside the arms you've
been given (to carry you). once you've reached this, you
have entered complete surrender. this may feel like a
combination of dream state/dehydration/self-deprecation &
    hungover
be present. surrender.   be okay with the fact that you
    fucking. just. can't.

Slide 7: The Archivist (57)

the chemist decides the variables have been jigsawed
decides this in the middle of the putting together
you hear the chemist crack you. make you fit. push you out.

pop.

in the middle of the putting together.

pop.

you get a glimpse of the chemist's fingers.
& she gives the thumbs down. needs to push you out more.

pop.
pop.

now more. incomplete.

pop.

now more. more.

pop.

a pen in her lab coat leaks slow like honey
& she smears the blue ink as if to sign her name.
you are her patent. her patient. her prayer's outcome.
a blueprint for floodgates in her waking dream.

all your splendor
& bedazzle based upon
how well you can cure a thing
mend a friendship or keep a lover

goddess   oh goddess   god
you must be purely exhausted
tired enough to slow your own heart rate down
& put yourself to death (if only fleeting)

to be a tiny raging goddess you must keep
your wings at ease
& your lightning rod lips from crackling

to be a huge sobbing goddess you must
keep your third eye rigid enough to see through
anyone's resilience
anyone's generational curse
anyone's honeycomb lies

Vintage God She Was (a)

as it was in the retro
when we were bellbottoms
on gods' hips

& we did not slop upon ourselves
& we did not smash our own
stones with our gem fingers

as it was when sheen
was afro & dap was not
an ornament

as it was we were the water
before any imbalanced ph
vaped our atmosphere for synthetic tears

as it was   before we was
    we just was

What the River Taught Me (Flow)

1. if you are the river
   you cannot drown (yourself).
2. motion is not the same as movement (move).
3. to be a waterfall, you have to fall.
4. there is submerge. there is emerge. there is merge.
5. a river can flow or trickle or crash on a rock or an
   eyeball or a throat or pussy.
6. waves are not apologetic or intuitive. just. present.

---

after the river, altar: honey, mirrors, yellow candles,
sunflowers, oranges, cinnamon, & 5 pennies

Acknowledgments

I am grateful for an attitude of gratitude when life and writing is good and flowing and when life presents seemingly unshakeable challenges. More importantly, I am grateful that I can depend on an unwavering higher source, ancestors by mission, vision or blood, spiritual practices, writing ancestors, and multiple pockets of supportive communities.

I am so grateful for Cave Canem, Hedgebrook, Ragdale, VONA, Mineral School, Y-WE, the Frye Art Museum, 4Culture, Artist Trust, and Jack Straw for providing spaces and opportunities for me to organize, channel, or write this work over time and recently.

I am grateful to writers who graciously let me borrow their eyes or ears in small and large capacities to serve as literary doulas to *Side Notes* and its many iterations: Daemond Arrindell, Rezina Habtemariam, Bettina Judd, Cynthia Manick, Natasha Ria El-Scari, Douglas Kearney, Tommy Pico, and Jane Wong.

Thank you to Dani Tirrell for widening the door to the "1980s" with "FagGod."

Thank you to living legacies: Toi Derricotte, Rita Dove, and Patricia Smith.

So much love and gratitude for my mother, roller-skating buddy, human reference book, and very first DJ, Barbara

North, for all the ways you've been rooting for me and affirming my love for art, poetry, music, and creativity. Never enough words to express my unconditional love and gratitude for my favorite squad: my children Brandin Tolbert and Indigo Tolbert and my life partner Naa Akua.

Lastly, deep gratitude to my brilliant editor, Jennifer Baker, for taking a chance on my work, reaffirming my wildest dreams, and her patience, and to Francesca Walker for her eyes, support, and loyalty.

Permissions and Credits

"Her Life (The Black Girl) in Unedited Episodes" [includes Pilot, Episode (24), Episode (16), Episode (27), Episode (7), Episode (12), Episode (23)], *Obsidian Literature & Arts in the African Diaspora*, What Tell Freedom Now, 2019, Vol. 45.2.

"Aunt Jemima Is the Picture of the American Dream" and "Low and Leaving," *Alta Journal*, 2020.

"Crest," *Crab Creek Review*, 2020.

"Shivering in the Summertime," *Catapult*, 2020.

Photo on page vii: Installation view of *Anastacia-Reneé: (Don't be Absurd) Alice in Parts*, Frye Art Museum, Seattle, January 30–April 25, 2021. Photo: © Jueqian Fang. Used by permission.

Photo on page 19: Courtesy of the author. Used by permission.

Photo on page 31: *Anastacia-Reneé: (Don't be Absurd) Alice in Parts*. Image courtesy of the author.

Photo on page 47: *Anastacia-Reneé: (Don't be Absurd) Alice in Parts*. Image courtesy of the author.

About the Author

Anastacia-Reneé (She/They) is a writer, educator, interdisciplinary artist, TEDx speaker, and the author of *(v.)* (Black Ocean) and *Forget It* (Black Radish Books). She was selected by NBC News as part of the list of "Queer Artists of Color Dominate 2021's Must-See LGBTQ Art Shows." Anastacia-Reneé was former Seattle Civic Poet (2017–2019), Poet-in-Residence (2015–2017), and Hugo House and Arc Artist Fellow (2020). Her work has been anthologized in: *The Future of Black: Afrofuturism, Black Comics, and Superhero Poetry; Home Is Where You Queer Your Heart; Furious Flower: Seeding the Future of African American Poetry; Teaching Black: The Craft of Teaching on Black Life and Literature; Joy Has a Sound; Spirited Stone: Lessons from Kubota's Garden;* and *Seismic: Seattle, City of Literature.* Her poetry and fiction have been published widely.